The Cherry Pie Incident

Brenda Short

This is a work of fiction. Any reference to people, places or events are creations of the author's imagination and any resemblance to actual events, places or persons living or dead is entirely coincidental.

Library and Archives Canada Cataloguing in Publication

ISBN 978-1-0691107-9-4 (pbk)

Short, Brenda, author

The Cherry Pie Incident / Brenda Short

Illustrated by Microsoft AI

Published by Doonhamer Publishing 2024

Dedication

To Julie Fox, tech wizard, my eternal gratitude for her assistance with this project and many others.

Preface

This is a fictional story about a greedy, narcissistic cat and an adventurous and hungry field mouse.

The story revolves around a freshly baked cherry pie that both of them find irresistible.

The baker is irate when she discovers that her pie has been contaminated by a rodent, and discards the pie in the trash can along with the mouse.

The mouse narrowly escapes being captured by the neighbourhood owl, but eventually the cat catches up with him.

Glossary

LeChat – The cat

LaMere – The mother

Souris – Mouse

Hibou – Owl

Quelle Horreur – How horrible

Children's books by this author

1. The Cherry Pie Incident
2. Noel and Sherlock
3. I'll Fix That Cat Later!
4. The Christmas Surprise
5. Frank's My Name
6. The Empty Nest
7. Easter Bunny has a fever
8. The Fishing Trip

The Cherry Pie Incident

"There used to be a certain pecking order in this kitchen, but now, nobody cares about convention. Rules are just ignored, and anything goes," sneered LeChat, the house cat, as he jumped off the kitchen table and ran over to the door.

"Where is it anyway, that nasty little rodent? It's been here. I can smell it…over here and over there, and..."

He stuck his nose into the dusty cracks and crevices in the door frame, searching for the mouse and sneezing fiercely in the process.

There was an established hierarchy in the food chain. Everyone was aware of it and as long as the minions didn't quibble, there was harmony in the kitchen. But suddenly here it was.

A serious breach of trust, a flagrant disregard for the kitchen protocol that LeChat had painstakingly laid down over the years, taking no prisoners in the process.

"Where is this upstart anyway?" he thought, cynically, "This...Souris, or whatever his name is. Well, I don't care how smart he thinks he is, he won't get away from me!"

He sauntered arrogantly out through the kitchen door and onto the porch, his long, silky fur almost floating around him and his tail whipping from side to side, demonstrating his mounting irritation as he sniffed the door jams in an effort to track down the trespasser.

Delicious, demonic thoughts of revenge floated through his head. What he would do when he finally caught the perpetrator of this, most heinous, insult! He licked his lips, as the thought of this made his mouth water involuntarily.

Last night, after a pleasant, though slightly bland supper of poached cod, LeChat was cat napping on his feather bed, lulled into a semi-conscious state by the sounds of baking.

The rolling pin was hitting the table in muffled thuds as LaMere rolled out the pastry aggressively.

Before long, she had worked one of her miracles again, finally producing a big, fat, cherry pie. Into the oven it went and soon began to emit an absolutely delicious aroma, hissing and spitting as it bubbled and baked, cherry juice spatters hitting the walls and floor of the hot oven in the process.

LeChat could already imagine how good this pie would taste, once it had cooled down of course, and LaMere always left her pies on the kitchen table to cool, giving him the chance to be the first to sample them.

He didn't really like the crust – neither the flavour nor the texture and anyway, if he ate it, he would have indigestion. So he didn't nibble on the pie, only licked up any juice that had seeped out of the crust.

Because of that, he left no clues behind, and LaMere had a clean edged pie – a veritable work of art.

If she only knew, LaMere would not appreciate the fact that he slobbered all around her precious pies, but LeChat had an arrogant streak a mile wide.

He assumed that the pies were baked for him. He was also extremely put out when they would suddenly disappear from the table during one of his frequent cat naps.

LaMere began to tidy the kitchen, cleaning up all of the dishes and baking tools, while LeChat dozed, patiently biding his time. She swept and then washed the floor, taking care to clean in the corners too, because she was hosting a luncheon the next day for her Quilting Club ladies.

When she had finished the cleaning, she stood her mop in the corner and moved the pie out of the oven onto the clean table as was her wont, leaving it there to cool.

Out went the kitchen light and LeChat heard her footsteps on the stairs that led up to her bedroom. The step at the top creaked, conveniently alerting him of her movements.

LeChat glanced over to the table, covetously anticipating his treat. Unfortunately, the cherry pie was still steaming, and he knew from experience that it would take a while to cool down enough for him to approach it.

A burned tongue was something you didn't want to repeat. He would have to wait…patiently…so in the meantime he might as well resume his nap...

Just after the clock struck the midnight hour, there was some activity in the far corner of the kitchen. An adorable, little field mouse had sneaked in from the garden and was surveying the perimeter of the kitchen, knowing full well that there was a predatory cat in the vicinity.

Souris was brave, but not stupid and would not put his life in danger lightly, but he was also hungry, not like the oversized, overweight, overindulged cat that protected this house and its perimeter.

The fragrance of the baking had escaped through the open kitchen window and saturated the immediate neighbourhood.

Souris had smelled the delicious aromas all the way from the far end of the garden, and being in desperate need of a good meal he decided to check it out.

The journey was fraught with danger and meant running the risk of being snatched up by Hibou, who patrolled the garden from the skies. Alternatively, he could be pounced on by the cat who seemed to sense his every movement.

But tonight, he was in luck. Hibou didn't appear and LeChat was sleeping. There were recurring nostril sounds that, although tiny and insignificant, were an indication of deep sleep.

There was also body twitching and tail slapping suggesting dreaming, so Souris took a chance and ran across the open expanse of kitchen floor.

With lightning speed, he reached the table leg and ran up to the top without stopping for a breath. Once there, he paused to reconnoiter.

Ah, yes! There it was! This is what he was risking his young life for. A huge cherry pie, all golden-brown flaky pastry and veritably oozing red, sticky juice.

This was heaven on a plate, and he was hungry enough to eat it all by himself, but he would have to be careful and leave no mess behind, or LeChat would know that he had been there first. That would really upset the big fur ball.

Souris clambered onto the pie, carelessly crumbling the edge of the pastry without realizing it, and leaving behind a telltale puddle of crumbs and juice that seeped from the newly created breach.

He walked slowly, carefully towards the centre of the pie, making his way along the lattice of pastry that LaMere had painstakingly woven, laying it on top of the cherries.

The purpose of this lattice was to let the steam escape when it was baking, and consequently was where many of the juice spatters had escaped.

However, it was also the perfect way for the little mouse to reach the centre of the pie.

He stopped on the edge, looking into an irresistible hole filled with plump cherries, suspended in thick, red juice. Souris was small enough to fit into this hole and carefully climbed inside, balancing on one of the cherries while he nibbled at the pastry from the inside.

After satiating himself with pastry and juicy cherry, he climbed out and crept quietly back across the pastry, dropping down onto the table, unaware that he was leaving behind tiny little footprints wherever he went.

He looked down at LeChat, who had changed his position and now lay on his back with all four paws suspended above his body.

Souris carefully observed his archenemy for a moment. Now was the perfect time to cross the floor, or else chance falling asleep right there on the tabletop. He was feeling drowsy and needed to find a hiding place to sleep off this veritable banquet.

Down the table leg and across the floor in a flash, Souris reached the floor mop without incident, just as LeChat twitched his paws and yawned long and wide, exposing those razor-sharp teeth with terrifying incisors…but he didn’t wake up.

Souris sneaked out through a tiny crack in the bottom of the door jam, almost becoming lodged in the space that had been adequately roomy when he originally sneaked in.

He crossed the lawn in a blur and reached the safety of the dense, overgrown hedge at the far end, but not a moment too soon.

Souris narrowly escaped capture by Hibou, who appeared from nowhere and swooped down on him just a moment too late to grab him in her talons. Phew! That was too close!

He disappeared under the hedge just as Hibou changed direction, losing some of her tail feathers in the top of the hedgerow.

Souris squeezed his roly-poly shape into his tiny nest, his belly a bit plumper than usual and his heart hammering in his chest.

He cleaned the sticky juice from his paws and face fastidiously before curling up in a ball, and went to sleep dreaming of delicious cherry pies and terrifying predators.

LeChat awoke to a terrible sound. LaMere was screaming and waving her hands, but he had no idea what had happened. The cherry pie seemed to be at the centre of this outburst and sure enough, LaMere picked up the pie, still yelling and stomped outside with it, tossing it in the garbage can.

"Oh, no! Wait a moment! Don't throw it away, I didn't have any yet," LeChat meowed plaintively.

He jumped up onto the table, in the hopes that there were some crumbs or a little juice that she had missed, and that's when he saw the incriminating evidence.

Tiny, red footprints crisscrossed back and forth on the table top, and of course there was that unmistakable odour of mice! Quelle horreur! That was a dead giveaway, and Souris would be made to pay the price when he finally caught up with him. Talk of the Devil!

Souris had taken the opportunity to sneak back in through the open door, hoping for some more of that delicious pie. He hid behind the mop, waiting for all the fuss to die down.

LeChat had just gone outside into the garden, with his tail slapping around. He

was obviously annoyed. Maybe he was in trouble with LaMere. She seemed to be very upset about something and was still muttering to herself.

Souris had no time left to wonder, as the mop he was crouching behind suddenly disappeared and caught him unawares, leaving him out in the open without cover.

LaMere screamed again as she came to the realization that she had a rodent infestation, this time swiping at Souris with the mop. She fiercely swept him up and flung him out into the garden, slamming the door shut behind him.

Once his head stopped spinning, Souris realized where he was and became a very happy mouse. He had landed in the garbage can and right on top of the newly discarded cherry pie.

Once more, he took his time and ate his fill of this sweet/sour deliciousness.

Eventually, he climbed out of the garbage can and wandered across the lawn, almost drunk with pleasure and completely satiated once more.

This would last him for a week. At least it might have done, but alas! It wasn't meant to be.

Suddenly and without warning, everything went wrong. Souris found himself trapped inside a veritable cage of razor-sharp claws. Hibou? No, he could smell cat! Either way he was in serious trouble.

LeChat grabbed this upstart mouse by the tail and tossed him up in the air. It was time to play with his breakfast, and what a nice breakfast it was. It was all plumped up with the cherry pie that he had been denied, but this would do as second best.

Souris looked down from a great height and saw his fate. A large mouth was waiting for him below, and the mouth was ringed with long, sharp teeth.

Souris had always had the benefit of speed on his side, but wasn't as clever as the cat. LeChat was smart enough to only lick the juice, and LaMere never caught him doing this.

Souris had infuriated the cat by being the first to eat the pie, but he had left his footprints behind along with crumbs and dribbled juice, and that had angered LaMere.

The pie had to be discarded, and that upset both of them all over again. However, Souris' plump, engorged, little body made a fine breakfast for LeChat who was finally able to savour his cherry pie, albeit indirectly, and gave it a thumbs up.

He would undoubtedly have indigestion all day from that unwashed field mouse and the contents of its stomach, including the pastry that always gave him such gas.

Everyone lost out today. LeChat lost his moment to taste test the pie, and of course LaMere wouldn't have the chance to impress her Quilting Club ladies.

The pie was a testament to her superior baking skills and she would have earned many compliments from the other ladies.

They were looking forward with great anticipation to sampling a slice of LaMere's famous cherry pie, but were presented instead with a disappointing plate of cookies, not even home-made, but from a packet no less! There had been no time to come up with a substitute.

By the following week the fiasco was now a thing of the past. LeChat was catnapping in the kitchen, lulled by the sounds and smells of baking once more.

LaMere had not allowed the cherry pie incident to dampen her enthusiasm for baking, but this time had decided to bake an apple pie.

"Mm. Oh dear…apple pie! Not my favourite," thought the feline gastronome as he sniffed the air. "The field mice can have the apple pie for all I care."

"That little pest was admittedly a pleasant distraction for a while. Something to look forward to, a natural enemy, prey for the predator…a real challenge!".

"If only I hadn't been so upset about the cherry pie! If only I hadn't acted so hastily and eaten the little rodent," he thought, regretfully.

"Souris was the best challenge of them all. He was so sneaky and clever…Pity! But life goes on," he thought, his remorse dissolving as quickly as it had arisen.

He flicked his tail in annoyance, and sneezed as his sensitive nostrils flared.

"Too much cinnamon!"

www.ingramcontent.com/pod-product-compliance
Lightning Source LLC
LaVergne TN
LVHW021351160826
845679LV00008B/1581